# A religious book

## Mister Bush Fire

authorHOUSE®

Information never before revealed to mankind

*AuthorHouse™ UK Ltd.*
*500 Avebury Boulevard*
*Central Milton Keynes, MK9 2BE*
*www.authorhouse.co.uk*
*Phone: 08001974150*

*First published by AuthorHouse 11/17/2009*

*ISBN: 978-1-4389-4668-9 (sc)*

*Printed in the United States of America*
*Bloomington, Indiana*

*This book is printed on acid-free paper.*

Lunar Colony  A fools errand
Iraq invasion by man eating super powers =
A war on God.
Mister Bush Fire = burnt this civilization.
Ultimate consequences = untold human misery.

# EXORDIUM

In order to kill Saddam Hussein, the man-eating superpowers dropped a 'bomb of democracy' on Baghdad. This action has in fact pulverised our world, the residence of Adam and Eve, and Christian civilisation is now suffering, having been dealt the thin end of the wedge. A scion of Adam, named GILLANI, complained to Adam and Eve against this evil deed, and Adam passed the case to Jesus Christ, who acts as Chief of Justice for the whole of Creation. The annual routine visit of Adam and Eve to Baghdad has been cancelled in view of this deliberately-inflicted chaos. Having being made aware of these human miseries, Jesus Christ is continuing to deliberate over the matter. He who was once crucified by this same flock, powerful in their numbers, is in the know as to how to deal with them properly.

The fire that erupted in Baghdad has now scattered to all parts of the globe in its remit, and burns fast and furiously wherever it touches. We call it MISTER BUSH FIRE. This book speaks about the global situation, informing mankind of the facts about the deliberate lighting of this all-consuming flame in order for the politicians to enjoy themselves.

In order to confirm the facts referenced in this book, readers are urged to consult the stack of U.N.O. records from before and after the Baghdad bombings.

This book also explains how Mister Bush Fire has been erasing our civilisation, resulting in terrible human misery in all parts of the world – there is more to this than meets the eye.

Jesus Christ, the hub of Creation, will soon manifest his miracle: the mortals' authoritarian democratic power will be vaporised by Mister Bush Fire.

# MR BUSH FIRE

The U.N.O is the outcome of political intellectuals endeavouring to maintain global peace, a guidebook to be followed by all nations for the removal of inhumanity and injustice. This government of the world is liable to keep the globe free from all underhand political trammels for the well-being of mankind. The U.N.O, comprised of all nations, is here to hold the scales even, but the fire of the Second World War has not been doused completely. It has been smouldering up to hodiernal developments in the name of wars (not the Great War): cold war, star war and arms war etc. They exhibit their dexterity in political threats, the mighty nations together cunningly making their wounds of war into a real war strategy, a war against a weak nation; a war between one tiny weak nation and all the mighty nations in the world. The tyrant war-mongers are barking at the tops of their voices - a war against a tyrant. This "holier-than-thou" expression has at last paid off handsomely. I am writing this religious feature in relation to the Iraq war undertaken by the Super Powers.

I have little knowledge of international political

intrigue, but I am steeped in religious belief - a "hardy annual" to have in modern politics.

I believe in the Almighty Creator, who made this world for it to be ruled by mankind. With this end in view the Almighty trained many messiahs and messengers to preach the divine line because He is the only Suzrain, a paramount lord of the universe. From time immemorial man has ruled the world by tribalism - DUUMVIRISM, TRIUMVIRISM, MONARCHISM - i.e. from all sorts of -isms to -CRACIES. These all now boil down to democracy, which has turned into an insidious disease for annihilation. This inescapable political method, for the first time in history, sowed the seed of inhumanity. Who did it? A burning question in politics? This is the outcome of horrid, inextinguishable desires that oozed out from the mighty nations that are subservient to the unscrupulous Super Power.

In a deterrent to global peace, after the Second World War the Super Powers became involved in the Vietnam war, in order to use harmful inventions to kill human beings. When this war ended in confusion, they fell into the trap of the Cold War. This world somehow skidded over it due to the fall of Marxism. When Russian and American leaders showed off their political half-nelson, many couldn't comprehend this ghastly outcome.

America is in a class of its own, able to do anything of its own free will because the coast is clear. This is a golden opportunity for America to target, unfailingly, the piping-hot oil product of producing countries. The U.N.O. and other world organisations are powerless to stand up against its brute force. America's skilful hunting at last came to fruition, and subtly they fried the Middle Eastern countries in their own oil.

It is easy to look at America with a jaundiced eye because of its global superiority. However, this country is not wholly responsible for the global ups and downs. The acme of its success stems from its acolytes.

To gain a plausible understanding, let us have a nutshell discussion of the Creation.

# ANTHROPOGENESIS

This universe is one of the products of God's immaculate creation. This world is the bone-marrow of creations; it has been a nest for human beings as a testing ground. When the world was completed He left it unused and uninhabited for many years, in order for it to be ready for the incoming super beings. This is the purpose of His creation. Through this intelligent being He would exhibit His attributes for His everlasting gratification. This is why man named Him Anthropomorphism.

When the world became fit for habitation, first of all He created engenuous (intelligent) beings out of the extract of fire, in male and female form, in order that they could propagate. These dawn men - non-Adamites - spawned throughout these continents and achieved the highest degree of menti-culture and civilisation. These synchro-flashing achievements reached their peak under the supervision of Eblis, a past master of creation who encouraged them to establish a galactic civilisation. When they were proficient at circling the square, Eblis admonished them to abide by the divine line. They took exception to this and treated his warning with an insubordinate attitude. After they had painstakingly searched across all the planets for a trace of God's existence, and confirmed nothing, they branded Eblis a liar. This resulted in an irreconcilable turmoil between Eblis and the powerful beings. They chased Eblis to murder him, but this attempt at murder was foiled; unknown to all, this polymath powerful being was immortal. After his escape, Eblis took this inextricably difficult issue to the Almighty for His resolution. Eblis was told to leave them to their own devices for the time being.

These meddling beings ruled this world for millions if not billions of years. Eventually they declared their complete denial of the Creator. God then commanded His War Minister, Israfeil, to uproot them by releasing a meteorite from his arsenal (a store of his W.M.D.). Israfeil, in accordance with the command of his supreme leader, did as he was asked and protected the good ones, and the operation was completed. The whole story is in the divine archive - a closed book of God.

That was a snippet of the earliest human creation, but a trace of this race will remain in the world forever. Evidence is waiting to be exhumed in order to solve the mystery by some kind of scientific research, for now and for all time to come.

As I am an ignoramus in science, from a religious point of view I do believe that the earth has gone through many phases in divine administration for the sake of man's trials and tribulations, in order to make it sublime. The Creator's real intentions are a great distance ahead of us at the present time. Mankind should consider it, for their own sake. This is an inexhaustible source of peace and happiness to be enjoyed. Every human soul has the right to imbibe this theory, so that he may practise it in his life.

# ISOMORPHIC ANTHROPOGENESIS

The multi-potent technological brute force is now gone from this world, although it did remain for millions of years. God left everything as it was, nothing new was created, while God's expertise was preparing the next chapter to come: beings more intelligent than the previous ones so as to mend the unhappy ending. God's creation, recreations and modifications have no end - an incomprehensible issue to human knowledge. The Maker knows best what to do next. He does nothing in compliance with the aspirations of mankind. He has a myriad of ways to create, which is an expugnable subject for the minds of all but a few human beings. When the mutations were completed, this time from the ones He had previously saved, He inspired the souls to aggrandise a new civilisation. As the years passed, they evolved to a higher stage by means of spiritual power. Again the world was illuminated to an amazing extent by their thoughts and technology, under the supervision of Eblis, the leader of all the angels. This removed global obfuscation by opening the door to human progression. These beings had unimaginable psychic power that they used to visualise and to trace out anything in the universe, when each part of His creation was not beyond their sights. God then sent Eblis to advise them not to surpass the divine boundary. Eblis did so accordingly but their cognition did not tally with the guidance of Eblis, because when they "scanned" the universe for signs of the existence of God, none were found. Their psychic search was more authentic than the previous one; they made all things immoral into human sexual relationships among parents, brothers and sisters. This world was encumbered with inexplicable sins because of hypocrisy, inequality and immorality. The members of this wealthy, impudent race were extremely proud of their acts of prurience; they depicted themselves committing all manner of sins. They threw out Eblis' admonishments completely in contempt, believing that the angel was seeking to glorify himself through the advice he was giving them. At this time wholesale slaughter was taking place all over the world - a world of two continents. The rest of the world had not yet been created. Geology, Physiography and the laws

of physics etc. were altogether different from those
of today.

# MODERN MANKIND

These puissant sexual perverts ruled the world for a myriad of men's years. It is the last phase of anthropology. Eblis up until now had been the guardian of human beings, and used to give accounts regularly to the Maker. One day, when the chaos had reached a peak, he told the Lord of the human misery; the Lord then commanded him to fetch a lump of soil for the solution of this human complexity. The Maker began to purify the soil by transferring it from one receptacle to another over a long period of time. Then He told Eblis that he would make a new race out of this extract of clay. Eblis entreated him not to create any more human beings because they are quarrelsome sexual perverts, a source of harm to this honourable creation. Eblis advised the Creator instead to make more angels, as they are sinless and obedient to Him. God told Eblis that he would never understand the ways of God. One day he made Adam, and proclaimed him to be the best of His creation, which went against the grain of Eblis who considered himself to be the best and the leader of all His creations.

This world was made to be ruled by mankind; if this were not the truth it would have been unnecessary to create humans. We call it a mystery of creation; the previous race before Adam was extirpated by the Maker who turned them into pigs and chimpanzees, except for a few good ones. God commanded the leader of the angels to show allegiance to Adam. Eblis refused - he was of the opinion that since Adam was made from clay, it was beneath his, Eblis', dignity to venerate Adam. After an altercation on this issue, the Supreme Being drummed him out of the divine palace, demoting him to the status of "the old gentleman". Eblis then prayed earnestly to God not to isolate him absolutely. As requested, God granted to him all evil powers.

Eventually Adam was sent to Iraq (Tigris and Euphrates), to develop his earthly way of life. He was soon out of his element, so some men from the previous race showed him worldly skills such as agriculture. Tigris and Euphrates were well-irrigated lands, well endowed with crops, an indispensable esculent for humans to live on. In this transitory world, the Grand Designer could not command the angels to instruct Adam on earthly life, as they are immortal creations and know nothing of the need for food and for sex. Adam and Eve were treated well by these people before them; the people demonstrated their obedience to Adam more than Eblis had done, which cheered the Maker. In later days, when Adamites saw the light of this world, he mingled those remaining from the previous race with the Adamites; thus He made mankind toe the divine line. From this premise we can understand that His previous creation was a not a lost labour. Mankind has emerged out of the first and out of the last (Adam). This modern race populated all parts of the world, so His earthly administration is going on in perfect order, managed by human beings.

# ADAMITES

Eblis had been waiting in the wings ready to lead the Adamites down the wrong path. He was infuriated when he saw things were slotting into shape. As the days went by after the departure of Adam, Eblis enticed mankind into sin. They were caught in a net woven by Eblis and baited by sexual misuse. Eblis knew that sex was the main theme in creation. It is a source of pleasure as well as misery. It is a source of creation and a weapon of mass destruction. In history, many pleasurable human developments have died away due to avoidance of divine sexual prohibition.

When Adamites mixed with non-Adamites, this world became polluted again. Then God, after preserving some good ones, washed them away, except for Noah and his family. Noah was the only survivor of the Adamites.

The scions of Noah filled in this world. The foremost scion is Jewish, and was the begetter of the new mankind, from whom God raised most of his authorised people, except Jesus Christ. The glory of God has been continuing glaringly as civilisation after civilisation rose and fell. History is fraught with pleasures and misery. Satanic power builds deviation to bring forth human misery.

This is now our world – a modern world. Adamites invented, explored, discovered this world – it did not happen in an instant. Thousands of years went by before mankind arrived at this stage. Human beings consist of esculent, soul, sex and brain. Other beings are without these indestructible qualities; this is why man is the best in creation. The human brain can bring forth bizarre faculties to perk up wisdom, knowledge and science in great amounts. The more they search, the more they will gain – it is boundless, limitless. The Creator endowed them with these astonishing qualities, to recognise His existence for obedience.

# CRIMINOLOGY

Now let us get down to brass tacks. Jesus Christ was sent to this modern world to proclaim the glory of God. His nativity was a turning point in the history of the world. He was put to death by hanging – by whom? Were they made from fire or from clay? It is a puzzle to decide who was who.

The fire-made scions had the tendency to commit crimes in disguise, or overtly to calumniate, satirize and defame the clay-made beings, because most of them were goaded on by the power of Eblis, who in collaboration with them made an evil plot against Jesus Christ, in order to cast the first stone in God's creation. They performed it gloriously; afterwards they were judged as criminals. The life of criminology did not come to an end here. After Jesus, when the prophet Mohammed came to this world, to perpetuate humanity and justice by cleansing the "Aegean Stables", the fire-made scions raised their ugly heads to send him to glory; but the plot against Mohammed did not come to fruition – he escaped, leaving Mecca for Medina. However, the criminals cherished the evil intention to wreak vengeance upon them. After the departure of Mohammed they quickly did this by murdering Kalip Omar and Kalip Osman. This is not the end, there is more to it. In order to sate their powerful blood lust, the criminals dragged it to Karbala, where a well-known history of hecatombs was made. This was in order to prove Islamic marrow, keeping the crust intact to etch on these words for the world's notice: "Islam is the best of religions".

This is Islamic indelible history as it ran up to the 16th century, when the reality was wiped out. It is not wise to return to the origin – the Dark Ages. The Almighty decided to endow it with some glory – to save the grace of His appointed representative we named it "Islamic civilisation of the prophet Mohammed"; however, this civilisation did not conform to Quoranic truth in the eyes of justice, so its entity was transformed into Christianity, who ran it up to the year 2000, when it was made into an illuminated civilisation for mankind. From east to west, no-one was left without its benefit.

What have we seen now? Two criminals – one is crucified, one is a Karbalic murderer.

After the year 2000, Muslim and Christian culprits were murdering human beings indiscriminately, to take over the global power for annihilation, as the two culprits carried on their illegal business under the name of religious politics. Their tortures, oppression, injustice and inhumanity reached their peak now under the mask of democracy.

They blame each other for their villainous acts. Both the Muslim and Christian killers claim to be men of justice – these fools have made this world what it is. They are chasing a mirage to drink water in vain.

These contemporary Muslim and Christian ruling ruffians are not Adamites who are existing in the realms. They cannot show their faces because of Satan's power. The Muslims who emanated from the race before Adam twisted Quoranic truths in such a manner that they were almost incomprehensible. Their mottos are Hajj, beards, prayers, mosques, madrasa, cutting off hands and cutting off heads. All these are given in the Quoran to understand humanity.

Muslims completely fired off humanity. They created a religion of human calamity and injustice. Sects and corruption flooded the world with these evils, and calumniated Allah's highly honoured messenger as "leader of the terrorists". These inexorable sins for all Muslims will continue. Non-Muslims are not liable for this sin, as they responded by having a slanging match with them.

# THE CHRISTIAN VANDALS

During the period of the Ottoman Empire, inhumanity reached its peak. The owner of the world entrusted global responsibility for Christianity under the aegis of Jesus Christ. This Christian civilisation flourished in all parts of the globe, irrespective of the high or the low. At the turn of the century the mighty nations wiped out all sorts of Biblical ways of life, thinking that due to scientific progression, religion had become a thing of the past. Now the balloon has gone up.

Who are they? Who inspired the abhorrence for religion? These people come from the fire-made beings made before the creation of Adam; also some Adamites mingle with them.

# CAN THE LEOPARD CHANGE ITS SPOTS?

## SADDAM HUSSEIN

Iraqi history was tainted by the genocidal rule of the Assassyn empire, coupled with indefinable Halukoo Khan's persecutions. Saddam Hussein was well-versed in this violent history before he took over the authority by a coup d'état.

Saddam considered that ruling with the rod was the only way to subdue the older sectarian violence that besmirched the Quoranic truth, in order to make peace-making history. When he rose in political eminence, the scions from those evil rulers stood against him, with a view to reserving their barbarous rule.

This time the anti-Saddam party, by means of intrigue, hit it off with a greedy Super-Power for sweet success. When Mr Bush, the inveterate Islamic-hater, came to power, in less than a week he had availed himself of the opportunity to welcome the intruders as "flowers in May", to wreak vengeance on Saddam because of his rumoured attempt to kill his father. His Pentagon expertise analysed each fawning course and realised how cunningly they could perform this task of annihilation, taking him for a fool. American politics can catch a weasel asleep – this is known by all students of political science.

The Pentagon-owner President is virtually the president of all weak nations in the world, and is able to twist them round his Pentagon finger. He has been an inventor of harmful technologies, especially since World War II. He could not manage to acquire all the powers under his umbrella, so he hit upon a plan – he would make unbreakable friendships with his past master, the global ruler, and the other puissant nations; then they must come to his aid, to make themselves into one voice big enough to gobble up a weak nation, like a tiger that has swallowed a lamb to satiate his hollow legs. With this malice prepense Bush killed Saddam. By pulverising the residence of the fountain head, he is immortalised through the killings of Kalukoo, Assassyn and Karbala. Bush ignored the real criminals.

# BAGHDAD BURNING

The President conversed about the burning of Baghdad with the British Prime Minister, as to how to perform this purge while keeping the rest happy with joviality. The leader of the British bunch devised astounding political shenanigans. Both agreed on this marvellous policy, and sent investigators to discover the whereabouts of Saddam and of the weapons of mass destruction (WMD). This entity of WMD sent shivers down the spines of Saddam's Muslim enemies around Baghdad. The hot-shot British leader flew off the handle when nothing of that ilk was found – he advised the President to start burning immediately. All their accomplices spoke with one voice, with due consideration. The most observant of all observers, the Prime Minister, worked hand over fist to start immediately and without fail in the name of democracy. Finally the puissant President gave the green light to burn Baghdad – we call it Mr Bush Fire ignited by the Pentagon.

I have seen on television pictures of a dreadful Australian bush fire – an inextinguishable fire which, after burning, is finally snuffed out by its own sweet will. All those fire-fighters are supposed to be killed because of their inability to find the WMD. Now the conflagration of Mr Bush Fire has been going on unopposed as the fire-fighters are thrown out. The world coast is crystal clear for the Pentagon. The powerful leaders are bubbling with mirth. The obsequious anti-party rights protesters dancing in the Baghdad streets are elated, especially the prominent rulers, along with their accomplices. The world is enjoying high jinks for the taste of democracy. The subdued upholders of human rights are giggling at Mr Bush Fire as all has gone as planned. The Iraqis are over the Baghdad moon. The inextinguishable Bush Fire has caused pleasures a-plenty.

The President has also aggravated the bush fire by unleashing unending Shia–Sunni violence, killings, lynchings and looting, all conspiring to turn Baghdad into a lagoon of human blood.

Millions burnt away, millions forced to leave their homes in order to find a haven in refugee camps. This is now a mega-bush fire under the title of democracy, this horrendous fire dispersing through the Middle Eastern petroleum countries ignited by oil. The flag of Mr Bush Fire is kissed by both America and Britain as a symbol of peace. The other mighty nations sit in an ivory tower smiling at the flag, trying to convince themselves that this planet is a better place without Saddam. They think they are on the defensive, whereas in fact, they are not – when the oil-rich countries are burnt out, where will the fire ignite next? You will know the answer better than I – you, the reader, are a consummate politician, to consume this planet and reduce it to ashes. An inextinguishable inferno, the fire has started to burn in every nation, either directly or indirectly. As for me, I believe Mr Bush Fire has burnt down civilisation root and branch – you cannot see the wood for the trees. Mr Bush Fire has a long way to go to evanesce himself after burning ashes have erupted, bringing harrowing human misery world-wide.

The U.N.O., the International Court of Human Justice, the British and American courts of justice – all of them kept the doors shut for fear of Mr Bush Fire. They are very aware of his evil force, which can penetrate anywhere. The Iron and Bamboo curtains will not be left alone. Time will tell!

# ORIGIN OF MANKIND

I am writing this religious article with regard to the Super Powers' invasion of Iraq.

How did life forms come into being on this planet? First the alpha and omega got the edifice made by His technicians as we do in our own residences. It took many years to complete it without any defects. After completion, He created intelligent beings to inhabit the planet and to come to know of the creation by their advancements. Similarly, here we do the same, so the question of man's evolution from monkey or pig is not logical. Here our source is from Adam and Eve who are mingled with the previous race. This is not a scientific view point – which may not be agreeable to that of religion. As I am ignorant in scientific matters, I am unconvinced about scientific theories; but for sure all scientific theories are not always correct.

# AFTER THE DEPARTURE OF ADAM AND EVE

When Adam and Eve departed from this planet, Eblis made Tigris and Euphrates (Iraq) the centre of his conspiracy to eradicate Adamites from the soil, because he had been turned into Satan by the Creator over the issue of Adam's creation.

Tigris and Euphrates (Baghdad) is the source of mankind – that is why he targeted it in order to fulfil his evil intentions. All strange calamities are here by his power. He collects his followers together to make a history of human misery for ostentation – to show how powerful he is. On the other hand, the Creator used the same place as a feeler to distinguish believers from unbelievers, Adamites from non-Adamites. From this premise you can now find differences among all nations, regarding who is who. The tricks of the "cunning old gentleman" are incomprehensible to most people. This is why I have tried to slant the facts of creation for general information, for my readers to know. What other alternative methods are there as a source of mankind – where has mankind emanated from?

There are many descendants of Adam in all parts of our planet – no country or nation, no inhabited piece of land is without their existence: they are in different forms of nations and religions.

This planet is made for that purpose – Adamites are destined to rule the world, for the purpose of peaceful management. As the fountain-head, he is the best of creation. If they cannot capture it, non-Adamites will hold the sway to ransack this impanation in creation, as they did before Adam.

# THE EXISTING CURSE OF TIME

At the moment, due to the state of carnage in Baghdad, we have discovered three adherents of the cunning Apollyon whose surname starts with a B. This does not mean all names that start with B are my objective – there are millions of people sharing this name who are unconnected with it. My favourite name begins with C = Christ = Crème de la crème

B = Bin Laden    = 1
B = Blair        = 2
B = Bush         = 3

No. 1 – the Saudi billionaire who has had financial investments in the countries belonging to no. 2 and no. 3. When the financial dealings were taken away he decided to take revenge – but how did he do this? No. 1 B was trained by no. 3 B. No. 1 B also showed his military dexterity in Afghanistan, which gave him the confidence to suppose he could take on the Super Power. He (no. 1 B) dreamed up a religious theory: "Islamic Jihad", which is in accordance with Muslim settlement in technology. Using Christian countries as a human shield is now forbidden. Thus his so-called Islamic Jihad bounced back to the honour of Allah's most favoured messenger Mohammed: it has disparaged the prophet as "leader of all terrorists". This is an inexpiable sin against all Muslims. Hajj, prayers beards, mosques and madrasa cannot rub out this black spot. All Muslims are liable to give account to the Court of Justice on the Day of Judgement. If no. 1 B finds fault with Christian countries, he must take his case to the U.N.O. for justification before uttering the words "Islamic Jihad", which has been used as justification for acts of terrorism. Some loathe this practice, but some are in favour as it has hoodwinked many Muslim intellectuals. The birthplace of the prophet, long known as a Muslim holy shrine, is now a hatching-place of terrorism. It has been transformed into a residence for Eblis, who was in dispute with the Almighty about the creation of the clay-made Adam, whose descendents (scions) would eventually become a nation of querulous individuals destined to spill blood on this planet. This prediction of Eblis had now come true. Can no. 1 B refute it?

# WHAT ABOUT CHRISTIANS?

Since 2001 the root of the Christian faith was torn out by the so-called politicians, priests and other so-called high-ranking Christian scholars. The churches have been broken in pieces by religious disarray in respect of sexual devaluation. Christian justice and humanity have been thrown out of the window by no. 2 B and no. 3 B. Since 2001 chaos, murder, disease, inhumanity and injustice have engulfed this globe. This is not just my pessimism, it is a sure way to eliminate the infrastructure of this planet – that fact is obvious.

# SPACE EXPLORATION

Oh, I have committed a faux pas! I have drifted from the main point – a spoonerism in my writing. My subjectivity is the flames of Mr Bush Fire. This fire has already burnt down this Christian civilisation now going up to the firmament. Since 1970 I have been in euphoria observing the human propensity in space exploration: we know success comes after trials and tribulations. This time science will open up a vista for galactic civilisation. This beaten path will one day release our pent-up desires for merriment. From Babylonian towers to N.A.S.A.'s burning desire, untold money has already been invested in this bizarre scientific experiment and inestimable amounts are still required to make it successful. Ebullient mighty nations are pouring into this excitable plan to make us happy. Space is already half full of scientific gadgets – science is progressing in leaps and bounds. Mr Bush Fire from Baghdad got hold of it to burn it up. It is unbelievable – I am sure you are thinking that a fire has no bearing on, say, lunar colonisation. As an unscientific man, probably my religious theory is nothing but gibberish; but now I am giving you a hint about how this lucrative business will turn into a "white elephant". Its ultimate consequence is nothing but a fool's errand because of Mr Bush Fire.

This entire creation is inter-linked in all its dealings. The Maker made it as such for mankind to ponder over its inexhaustible source of erudition. So Mr Bush Fire is a man-made disaster, and is begetting natural disaster, as nature is inter-linking with man's way of life, and the laws of physics are conceding to this theory.

The Supreme Grand Designer made all living things in male and female order, but the enchanting creation of Adam and Jesus Christ is out of His established process. They are created out of His power source for particular spectacular reasons.

# DON'T KEEP A MAN AND WORK YOURSELVES

This statement relates to the creation of Adam and Jesus Christ. The Almighty has entrusted the responsibility of His creation to them. They are in charge of its administration; so God does not keep a man and work himself. It is a similar process regarding the administration of the world – you can understand it easily if you consider human constitutions in the various departments that run the affairs.

Adam of Baghdad and Christ of Nazareth are the heads of his entire management, including all planets and sub-planets. Mr Bush Fire, after burning Christianity, shook hands with Islamic vandals for the burning of Baghdad, the residence of Adam. Do you think he will allow these ruffians to take over the moon, when they are holding a Pentagon to his head? The lunar colony will lie in the figment of imagination - the usurpers will be punished.

Mr Bush Fire, in consequence of "War on Terror", burnt the culture, along with the heavenly "Pandora's Box", to a frazzle. Scientists and physicists are sanguine about casting an anchor to the scientific windward, now that we see which way the wind blows. The copper-bottomed investments will cut a sorry figure in the long run, because the bottom has been burnt by Mr Bush Fire. Time is not far off for them to be jumped out of their skins.

These Three Bs, the obviously outstanding global terrorists and their accomplices, need to be exterminated in order to make the planet a better place to live in.

Who will do it?

The real Adamites. To know them, read "Terro Jihad".

Coming soon:

1. Evolution (the theory that man evolved from animals is a scientific load of bull)

2. How God makes and rules (God did not create this universe by himself)

3. God the Grand Designer (Moses did not converse with God on Mount Sinai)

4. Another Ugly facet of democracy (Jesus Christ is the only peacemaker)

5. Brass Tacks (Absence of God on Judgement Day - Jesus the resurrector, the last day - The first day)

Information never before revealed to mankind